Raising
Right-Hearted
Kids
in a
Wrong-Way
World

Raising Right-Hearted Kids in a Wrong-Way World

Pastor David Rosales

Raising Right-Hearted Kids in a Wrong-Way World

*Dedicated to those special ones
who have blessed my life...*

To my parents, Frank and Bonnie Rosales, who
have remained faithfully married and in love for
over 51 years, loving their children with all their
hearts. Standing by me in all I have done, you
have tremendously influenced my life by your
love and devotion.

To my beautiful and loving bride,
Marie—you are my greatest love outside of
Jesus. My dearest friend and most cherished
companion, you have always been there for me.
Thank you for your committed love to me.

To my precious children, Carin Marie,
David Aaron, Joseph Andrew, and Anna
Rebekah, who have been the love of my life
since the day I knew their mom first carried
them in her womb. My children, I love you with
all of my heart, and pray that Jesus will always
be your greatest love. In all of your pursuits,
seek Him first and your life will be complete.

And finally, to my pastor Chuck Smith
and his wife Kay, Marie and I thank you for
your dedication to Jesus and your love for us.
The two of you have meant so much to us over
so many years. We love you dearly.

Contents

Raising Children for Jesus . . .

Raising children for Jesus—what a simple thing to say. Although most Christian parents would probably agree that it is one of the most challenging tasks we will ever face. There are so many forces aligned against our children today, let alone their own nature. Nevertheless, the Lord has given us the privilege and responsibility of raising them in the nurture and knowledge of Him.

As a father of four, I would have to say that I have not arrived. I have made more mistakes than I care to remember. Considering this, I feel completely unqualified in writing a book such as this one. Yet perhaps some of the things I have learned over the years may help others who are also on this journey. This book is not written as a you-can't-lose-with-the-methods-I-use mentality; rather it should be viewed as a voice echoing the desires of so many Christian parents. We love our children and want the best for them, always.

I cannot help but remember the tragic passage found in the second chapter of the book of Judges. In this passage, the people of Israel have been rebuked for their lack of complete obedience to the Lord. The Bible records a very sad commentary on what occurred in Israel at that time. Judges 2:7–10 reads:

> So the people served the LORD all the days of Joshua, and all the days of the elders who outlived Joshua, who had seen all the great works of the LORD which He had done for Israel. Now Joshua the son of Nun, the servant of the LORD, died when he was one hundred and ten years old. And they buried him within the border of his inheritance at Timnath Heres, in the mountains of Ephraim, on the north side of Mount Gaash. When all that generation had been gathered to their fathers, another generation arose after them who did not know the LORD nor the work which He had done for Israel.

As a card-carrying member of the early 1970's Jesus Revolution, I have seen firsthand how people who were saved in those wonderful days have often failed to communicate their faith to the next generation, their own children.

With this in mind, I have written this book. It is written with the hope that we will successfully impart our faith in God through His Son, Jesus, to our children. It is also my desire to encourage you to "be ready, for the Son of Man is coming in an hour you do not expect Him." May God bless you as you endeavor to be faithful in one of the most important tasks you have been called to as parents—the task of leading your children to Jesus Christ our Savior.

I believe that with the Lord all things are possible, and that we can successfully lead our children to Jesus, helping them to develop character and faith in God. It's not easy, but it is possible. Hang in there, for one day your children will indeed rise up and call you blessed.

May God be with you, strengthen you, and give you wisdom as you serve Him.

The Gift He Has Given

Behold, children are a heritage from the Lord,
the fruit of the womb is His reward. Like arrows
in the hand of a warrior, so are the children of
one's youth. Happy is the man who has his
quiver full of them; they shall not be ashamed,
but shall speak with their enemies in the gate.

—Psalm 127:3–5

Indeed children are God's gifts to us. This was hammered home to me years ago when I took my family on a trip up to Morro Bay. My son, David, was just a little guy—I think he was two or three at the time. Little David used to run around the house wearing his Superman cape. First it started as a dishtowel, and then a rag, ultimately resulting in his Aunt Pattie buying him the actual costume. She recognized his strong fascination with the adventures of Superman and all that comes with little boys' imaginations. He was in heaven.

He proudly wore his new cape fastened around his neck with a big red "S" on his chest. With it on, David ran around the house, arms extended, his little blue cape blowing behind him. SWISH—SWISH—you would hear as he passed by your feet. Marie and I were constantly tying that cape on him. He ate with it on, slept with it on, and if we had let him, he would have bathed with it on. Seeing how important it was to him, we let him wear it all over the place.

One day, Superboy, his mom, his older sister and I went on vacation to Morro Bay. We stopped at a little park to visit a museum. This particular museum had an incline driveway. As you would ascend the driveway, you had to creep along very slowly, for at a certain point the nose of your car would rise above the level parking lot making it impossible to see ahead.

When we arrived at the museum, Marie and Carin left to buy tickets, while Superboy stayed with me. I had to get something from the trunk, so I turned to Davie and said, "Honey, stand next to Daddy." As I opened the trunk, I heard tiny footsteps running away. I quickly turned to see David running across the parking lot right as a car was traveling up the driveway. I knew the woman could not see my son, so I screamed his name at the top of my lungs, "DAVID—STOP!" Immediately he stopped. The car stopped at the same moment. My heart froze in my chest. Then it hit me. *I could be burying this little guy in his Superman cape next week.*

I took him behind the car and applied the board of education to the seat of understanding, speaking to him with great emotion about how he needed to obey by staying next to Daddy. The Lord impressed upon me that day something which has driven me since then. He said to me, "If that little fella were to have been taken today, what would you have given him? What did you invest in his life that was of value?" I came to realize that the only thing I can give my children that is of any worth is my faith in Jesus Christ. That's it.

Right about that time, a song was very popular that spoke of a father's relationship with his son. Even though it is a secular song, the Lord used it in my life. Basically, it is the story of a man who never made any time for his son. He constantly put his son off, saying, "We'll get together then, Son." And, of course, "then" never came. The song ends with a line that pierces my heart. Realizing his inadequacy as a father, the dad tries to make up for lost time, so he asks his son if he could visit with him. But his son, just as he had done for so many years, made up excuses saying he was too busy. Hanging up the phone, the dad says, "My boy is just like me."

Both of my sons, David and Joseph, expressed to me when they were young that they wanted to be like me. David loved to play catch with me. When he had a baseball game, he would stand over the plate with his bat looking for just one person in the stands—Dad. If I were unable to make it to a game, David would be sad. On one occasion, when I was preparing to go to the Philippines for ministry and could not make it to a game, David asked me to come watch him play basketball during his lunch break. I went. I stood and watched him the entire hour because I knew how much it meant to him.

I must admit, the words to that song rang through my head. I purposed in my heart not to let that happen to my son and me. Even though I made that determination a long time ago, I still wrestle with the thought, *Am I doing enough*? Being a parent is trying, is it not? Yet nothing is more rewarding than being there for them. If one day one of my babies turns to me and says, "Daddy, you weren't there," I will be able to say, "No. I was there. I was always there." After your spouse, your children are the most important relationship in your life. Take care of them. Be there for them; they will not be home forever.

I pray for the parents in my church because it is tough to find a proper balance with life's demands. I really believe the enemy works overtime in believers' lives. On one hand, you want to give your kids as much attention as possible. On the other hand, if you are not careful, they can become idols. When your baby does not want to go to church, you do not go. If your child does not like the Sunday school teacher, you move to another church. However, if you continually try to make life easy for them, saying, "I'll go some place where they treat my child better," you may be in danger of choosing to please the child instead of pleasing the Lord. Maybe it is time to spank them, but you avoid it because it is taxing on you. Believe me, there have been many times when I have disciplined my children and afterwards it brought tears to my eyes. Parenting the right way is not easy, but it is essential.

One woman from the Bible who truly inspires me is Hannah. She serves as an excellent role model for parents by her love for children and her devotion to the Lord. Hannah could not have children, which was a great burden to her. One day, as she prayed in the tabernacle with a fervent heart, the high priest, Eli, caught sight of her. As he watched Hannah praying, he saw that her lips were moving but no sound came forth. Immediately he thought that she was drunk, so he approached her and rebuked her for being drunk in the tabernacle:

> "No, my lord," she exclaimed, "I am a woman of sorrowful spirit. I have drunk neither wine nor intoxicating drink, but have poured out my soul before the Lord. Do not consider your maidservant a wicked woman, for out of the abundance of my complaint and grief I have spoken until now." Then Eli answered and said, "Go in peace, and the God of Israel grant your petition which you have asked of Him"
>
> —1 Samuel 1:15–17

God answered her petition, and she had a child. Her response was, "For this child I prayed, and the LORD has granted me my petition which I asked of Him. Therefore I also have lent him to the LORD; as long as he lives he shall be lent to the LORD."

Is this your response? Perhaps at times you have said, "Lord, this gift you've given to me, I don't understand him." Or, "Why this gift, Lord?" Our prayer should really be "Lord, precious is this life you've given to me, and I give him back to you."

If you are struggling to understand your place as a parent, let me encourage you to put your child in the Lord's hands. He or she is God's creation, His gift to you in this life. And as much as we love our children, parenting is still one of the most difficult responsibilities we will face as human beings.

Because rearing a child for Christ is so complicated, obviously we will not do everything right. We may want a batting average of a thousand, but we never will. We are going to make mistakes. The Lord knows this, but this can be hard for us to face. Our best hope is to make good choices most of the time; and, with God's help, try to bring our children into a real, active relationship with Jesus Christ. I am aware of the fact that I am incapable of being a perfect parent, so I must constantly seek the Lord for His wisdom because He understands my children completely. Presently, my children are ages twenty-two, twenty, eighteen, and sixteen. Although I have already been through quite a lot, there are still a number of things I have yet to go through with my children.

Proverbs 15:22 states, "Without counsel, plans go awry, but in the multitude of counselors they are established." Often I learn from talking to other Christian parents, who have gone

---

through similar situations or trials. I do not claim to have all the answers. I stand as a man who is doing the best that he can, with the Lord's help. God has graciously given me wisdom and counsel over the years, which I want to share with you; things that I hope will help you as you endeavor to bring your children to Christ.

Leading Your Child to Christ

He will feed His flock like a shepherd; He will gather the lambs with His arm, and carry them in His bosom, and gently lead those who are with young.

—Isaiah 40:11

Raising children is rigorous. Once you have figured out how to get little Johnny to put his toys away, ten new areas spring up that you need to teach him. It is a 24-7 task: twenty-four hours a day, seven days a week. There are no vacations. No breaks. No substitutes. It is a job that never ends, and, at times, it can be overwhelming.

Under the pressures, some people throw their hands up in the air, crying, "I give up!" And that is exactly what Satan wants each of us to do. He wants us to try parenting in our own strength, believing we can do it on our own. But the truth is, without the Holy Spirit we will eventually wear ourselves out or merely slip away from our children, busying ourselves until we are no longer an instrument of influence in their lives.

Parents often ask me, "David, what am I supposed to be doing? How can I become a better parent? How can I make up for my mistakes?" Of course, there are no simple answers to questions such as these.

Having been a father for over twenty years, I have traveled down this road for quite some time, but I certainly do not consider myself an expert. A lot of times, I think I fail more than I succeed. Like you, I am a pilgrim on this particularly challenging journey, and I am trying with all my heart to do it right. In spite of my weakness, the Lord is faithful. He takes me by the hand and guides me down the path of parenting as it unfolds before me. So when someone asks me, either as a pastor or a friend, where to go to find answers, I always begin at the same place—the Word of God. The answers to all of our questions as parents are found here, for it holds instruction in every area of life. I may fail, but God's Word never fails.

As Moses sought to instruct the Jews in their relationship towards God, it is evident that raising children was an issue even in his time. Moses not only gives parents direction concerning their own relationship with the Lord, he instructs them in how to train up their children as believers:

Hear, O Israel: The LORD our God, the LORD is one!

You shall love the LORD your God with all your heart, with all your soul, and with all your might. And these words which I command you today shall be in your heart; you shall teach them diligently to your children, and shall talk of them when you sit in your house, when you walk by the way, when you lie down, and when you rise up. You shall bind them as a sign on your hand, and they shall be as frontlets between your eyes. You shall write them on the doorposts of your house and on your gates.

—Deuteronomy 6:4–9

For many centuries the Jews have known this passage from Deuteronomy as the Shema, reciting it as a daily prayer for generations. The Shema reveals the Jewish understanding of God, that He is wholly unique and, therefore, He alone is to be worshipped. It also yields four specific truths for parents to use in attempting to lead their children to the Lord. If we want to impact our children for Christ, we must assimilate these truths into our hearts and minds:

1. You must have a personal relationship with Jesus Christ yourself.

2. You must be openly and totally committed to Jesus Christ.

3. You must be committed to evangelizing your children.

4. You must build your home into a sanctuary.

YOU MUST HAVE A SAVING FAITH IN JESUS CHRIST

We can not expect our children to know and follow the Lord if we do not have our own personal relationship with Jesus Christ. The Lord is to be the sole object of our affections. This is the message that Moses delivered when he spoke these words from the Shema: "Hear, O Israel: The LORD our God, the LORD is one." By stating that the Lord is "one," Moses is teaching the Jews that they can have no other gods. This is true for us today. God invites us to have a personal relationship with Him through His Son, Jesus Christ.

When Moses addressed the Israelites with this life-changing message, the world in which they lived was filled with paganism and polytheism. In fact, the Israelites had begun to chase after all sorts of idols and pagan gods. Seeing this, God graciously stepped in by giving Moses the Shema, declaring that the Jews were to have an uncompromising relationship with the King of Kings and the Lord of Lords. God's message to the Israelites was plain and simple: He alone is God, and He never wants them to forget it. Therefore, after Moses delivered these words to the Israelites and their hearts were turned back to the Lord, the Shema became Israel's cry of allegiance to God. For generations it has been the Jews' daily practice to utter this prayer aloud; for in rehearsing it, their children learn who God is and how to worship Him. Also, through its recital, Jewish parents pass on their love for the Lord to their children.

Like the Israelites, we need to repeatedly declare our commitment to the Lord, encouraging our children to know Him. I discovered a long time ago that the only God my children will be acquainted with is the God that lives inside of their father and mother. When my children were small I took advantage of how they looked up to me. Once my son, Joseph, said, "Dad, you could beat up Mike Tyson, couldn't you?" Of course, I let him think I could. When kids are young they look at you as if you are the greatest person on the planet. To them, you are. However, faith in Jesus Christ needs to be what they see in you so they will learn that He is the Greatest.

As they grow older, they may say, "My dad isn't perfect." Most likely they will have reams of memories when dad was not perfect. What can you do? You have to leave yesterday alone and live for today. Certainly you will make mistakes, but it is how you deal with your mistakes that will truly affect your children. As we live by grace, we teach our children that God is full of grace. I thank God that every day is a new day. His mercies are new every morning. We can not let the past interfere with what God wants to do right now. Keep your eyes on the goal—the salvation of your children—not on your failures.

YOU MUST BE OPENLY AND TOTALLY COMMITTED TO JESUS CHRIST

Deuteronomy 6:5 states, "You shall love the LORD your God with all your heart, with all your soul, and with all your might." How can you openly and sincerely demonstrate your faith to your children? First, love God with all your heart. "Heart" speaks of your life's priorities. What is your heart set on today? Is it a new car? A new job? Perhaps, it is to climb the ladder-of-success. Whatever it is, I'm sure your kids could tell me if I were to ask them. From time to time it is good to assess your priorities, bringing your heart before the Lord. He is faithful to show us when we stray from His will. Humbling ourselves is the first step in realigning ourselves with our Master's priorities.

Words reveal what makes up the heart. Matthew 12:34 says, "Out of the abundance of the *heart* the mouth speaks." What flows from your mouth? Are your words edifying or destructive? Ask the Lord to put a guard over your mouth and to give you words that will uplift and encourage your children.

Second, love God with all your soul. "Soul" refers to your spiritual appetites. Do you hunger and thirst after God? As your soul rests in the Lord, all your spiritual needs are met in Him. Then as your children watch you, their young souls will be impressed to seek God for refuge.

I once read about a man who had a long relationship with the Lord. When he was in the hospital about to die, a minister entered his room to visit him. Beside the man's bed the minister noticed an empty chair. He asked the man if someone had come to visit him. Smiling, the old man replied, "Jesus sits there and talks to me." A puzzled expression covered the minister's face, so the man explained, "Years ago a friend told me that prayer was as simple as talking to a good friend. So everyday I pull up a chair, invite Jesus to sit on it, and we have a good talk." Some days later, the daughter of this man came to the parish to inform the minister of her father's death. "He seemed so content," she recollected, "So I left him alone in the room for a few hours. When I returned, he had died. But I did notice something strange. His head was resting on an empty chair beside his bed."

Are you resting in the Lord? Nothing speaks louder to a child than the quiet, restful soul of a parent. If you want your child's soul to be at rest, you need to lead by example, "casting all your care upon Him, for He cares for you" (1 Peter 5:7).

Lastly, love God with all your might. "Might" refers to your physical labors. Your work, your play—all that you do should be done for Him. "You are our epistles written in our hearts, known and read by all men," wrote Paul to describe the Corinthians' role as ministers of the New Covenant. Likewise, our children read our lives as words on a page. We are accountable for our actions. As we travel down the road of life, we need to consider where we are leading our children.

If asked, what would your children say is the most important thing in your life? Maybe thinking about it makes you uncomfortable, but it is important to consider. If we want our lives to impact our children for Christ, we have to live like we do. You are His handpicked witness to your children.

YOU MUST BE COMMITTED TO EVANGELIZING YOUR CHILDREN

The third element we see in Deuteronomy is a commitment to evangelism:

> And these words which I command you today shall be in your heart; you shall teach them diligently to your children, and shall talk of them when you sit in your house, when you walk by the way, when you lie down, and when you rise up. You shall bind them as a sign on your hand, and they shall be as frontlets between your eyes.
>
> —Deuteronomy 6:6–8

I may travel the world and see many souls saved through the ministry, but if my kids are unsaved I have failed. Billy Sunday, a great preacher, once said that even though he had led thousands to the Lord, the tragedy of his life was that his own two sons were unbelievers. I am trying to avoid such a tragedy. My home is my church and my kids are my congregation. My children need to be saved; therefore, they need to be evangelized.

Our goal for evangelism has always been for our children to discern the truth for themselves. The Easter our son, Joseph, was ten years old, his third-grade class had to make a card—guess what he drew on his card? He drew the Easter Bunny on its knees in front of the tomb of the resurrected Christ.

When he was born I held him in my hands, and speaking out to God, I said, "This one is the preacher." Having prophesied over him then, I now see in him a heart of compassion, a love for Jesus, and a zeal for evangelism. I never told him, "The Easter Bunny has to worship Jesus." His picture originated from the Spirit of God. To this day whenever I think about it my heart leaps with joy.

Some Christians have bought the world's view, saying that too much of the Bible may cause your child to rebel. Nothing is further from the truth. One of the reasons why kids rebel is that they see hypocrisy in the lives of authorities, or because no one has established authority in their lives. Do not hesitate to evangelize your children. Creatively use every waking opportunity to teach your children about Christ. Pray for the Lord to sustain you if you are weary, but never, ever give up.

YOU MUST BUILD YOUR HOME INTO A SANCTUARY

"You shall write them on the doorposts of your house and on your gates" (Deuteronomy 6:9). Is your home a sanctuary, a safe place from the world? Securing our homes for Christ is becoming increasingly difficult. If we neglect to monitor the television shows our children watch, the images they view on computer screens, the music they listen to, and the print they read, then we have failed to secure our homes. Monitoring means involvement—an extensive effort on the part of the parent. Do you really know what is being fed into your child's mind? If we do not monitor what they do, as well as instruct them in the Lord, how will they be trained to discern God's ways from the world's ways?

Parents, you need to find a replacement for whatever may be drawing your child away from the Lord. Train your children to "put off" their worldly nature and "put on" the nature of God. Spiritual principles need to govern our lives and theirs. Fathers, read the Word of God to your children. Pray with them and for them. Lead devotions with your family. Mothers, if you are not married to someone who will lead, then do it yourself. Do unto the Lord, praying that your husband will catch the vision. If your husband is not saved, continue to pray for him, but do not lose time training up your kids for Christ. Their eternal salvation is at stake.

WALKING IN YOUR FOOTPRINTS

Back when my son Joseph was only a toddler, I had gone out to my backyard, which was all torn up because I was in the process of replanting the lawn. I remember it like it was yesterday. As I hurriedly crossed the yard, a strange little noise caused me to pause and look over my shoulder. Without my realizing it, little Joseph had followed me into the muddy mess. Joey's little throat made grunting noises as he strained and stretched his small legs, trying to place his footprints into mine, step for step. I asked him, "What are you doing?" as a broad grin covered my face. Looking up with his big brown eyes, he said, "I'm walking in your footsteps, Dad." At that moment the Lord spoke to my heart: Your son is walking in your footsteps. Where you go, he will go. What you love, he will love. Your God will be his God. Keep that in mind.

Our children walk in our footsteps. Since that day I have kept this lesson in mind. As youth, they are impressionable, so we are wise to pour as much into their lives as we can. In the home, I display my faith by explanation and example. Not only do I have to talk the talk; I have to walk the walk. Your children are going to learn how to live by watching you: how you worship, how you serve, how you give, and how you relate with the Lord, Jesus Christ. You must decide to wholeheartedly live for the Lord. No more compromise. No more letting things slip a little bit here and there. Early training has distinct ramifications in a child's life. The impression you make on them by loving and serving Jesus will last a lifetime.

What the World Says About Children

But whoever causes one of these little ones who believe in Me to sin, it would be better for him if a millstone were hung around his neck, and he were drowned in the depth of the sea.

—Matthew 18:6

This present generation is caught up with the pursuit of personal satisfaction, but what they are not aware of is that such pursuits will ultimately destroy it. In fact, the majority of people consider the pursuit of happiness to be a God-given right. They teach it to their children, perhaps willfully, but mostly by example. In order to train a child—in order to have a successful home life—children must learn how to sacrifice and how to be selfless. These virtues are not learned by words alone. They need to be lived out. Unfortunately, we are in a generation that is raising its children with no sense of priorities, without any sense of sacrifice or selflessness.

In most instances, whatever the worldly belief is at the time, the opposite holds true for Christians. For example, many years ago, I was enrolled in a Marriage and Family class at Cal Poly Pomona. I will never forget that class, especially two ladies who sat in the front row. From their seats at the front of the room, they made it a habit to interrupt the professor and impose their views on the rest of the class. Both were feminists, very aggressive, opinionated, hard-to-deal-with ladies. Because of their aggressive approach, they practically took over the class. To make matters worse, when one of the ladies interrupted, the professor never attempted to take control. Needless to say, my frustrations ran high.

Several weeks into the quarter, the class was dealing with the topic of raising children. I posed the question: "If a child is raised in a home where both the mother and father work full time, isn't it true that he is going to have a sense of diminished value because both mother and father don't seem to care enough to give him any time?" As soon as I had asked my question, one of the two ladies turned to the professor, saying, "May I answer that question?" By that time I had grown tired of this woman answering everybody's questions. I turned to her and said, "If I wanted to know what you thought, I would have asked—but I didn't, I asked for the professor's opinion." She became quiet immediately; however, the second lady turned to me, growing increasingly louder as she voiced her thoughts on the matter. As you can imagine, things really began to heat up. For the remainder of class conversation was really interesting. Actually, it was one of the best discussions our class had all semester.

Those two ladies were so filled with worldly philosophies that it came out every chance they could get. I have noticed that when I bring up similar questions with worldly people, they react with anger. Their voices climb as they defend themselves, insisting that working fulltime does not adversely affect their children. This does not surprise me. I expect the world to react this way. But when I say to the church, "Ladies, your responsibility is not to be a bread winner but a mother," parents react like the world does—they are offended.

Somewhere along the line a lot of parents have been sold the lie "You can have it all!" But you cannot have it all. You have to make a choice. If you want to do it all and have it all, you will have guilt and an ulcer. Plenty of people, including Christians, operate by the world's system of selfishness. Instead of raising their children in a godly environment, influencing them to make a decision for Jesus Christ, they have chosen the boat, the house, and the cars. Believe me, the boat is not worth it, neither is a house or a car—no material possession is worth the time you should be investing in your child's life. What do you value? Are they God's values?

Today children are facing decisions that some of us never had to make. We need to establish priorities and teach them to our children. This young generation is under tremendous pressure. Often times, kids battle pressures without mature guidance. Peer groups become "the parents" when mom and dad are not actively involved. Kids listen to friends over their parents because pleasing friends becomes their top priority. If mom and dad do not show an interest by knowing who their kids' friends are—or where they are going, or what they are doing—then mom and dad have basically vacated their positions. What they are saying is, "Go ahead, do whatever you please because I don't have the time." As long as we continue treating our children this way, this generation is going to be a generation without God.

THE CHOICES CHILDREN ARE MAKING

Children are forced into making decisions about sex, drugs, and recreational activities more frequently than past generations— and they are paying far greater consequences for their mistakes. These kids need to be protected, not left alone.

Consider the war on drugs, for instance. In the 1960s, very few people from my high school took drugs. In fact, there were so few of us that the teachers knew exactly who we were. We would go out at lunchtime, drink, smoke marijuana, and then go back to class with our sunglasses on because our eyes were so bloodshot. We wandered around the campus stoned, and everyone knew it. We were a minority back then. Today's world is far different. For the majority of kids whether to take drugs is hardly an issue. The question now is which drug to take and when.

In an effort to stop this assault on our children, educators and politicians have implemented programs telling kids "DARE to say no!" Not given a reason to say no, they are told to say it anyway. On the other hand, Christian kids can say, "I have something better than drugs—I don't need your drug." They have Jesus Christ, who has given them power over sin. The world has nothing like that to offer. Without anything stronger than drugs, kids take them.

Sexual promiscuity is another area where children are being attacked. "When" to have sex is being pushed, but the "why" is being left out. Adolescents' greatest concern seems to be having intercourse, rather than waiting until one is married. Girls wonder whether they should have intercourse on the first date or the second. Sadly, mom and dad often are left out of the decision making process. Parents expect schools to teach their kids "safe sex," when there is no such thing as safe sex. If it is not in the confines of a monogamous marriage, it is always dangerous, destructive. When educators or parents tell kids that "sex is safe when they use a condom" or "only sleep with someone that you love," they are telling kids a lie. How many people were you in love with at age thirteen? fourteen? fifteen? I know I was "in love" with a lot of people at those ages. To tell kids that its OK is a lie of the world—straight from the mouth of Satan.

How about clothing today? Because peer pressure is everything to kids, to wear clothing that is "in" is more important than to wear clothing that is modest. Parents need to shop with their kids, spending time with them to make sure that they know the importance of being modest and not becoming a stumbling block to others. Not taught the value of the dollar, some kids do not care if a pair of tennis shoes costs $125. You can give a kid $300 and say, "Go out and buy some clothes," and he will come back with a pair of tennis shoes and a few T-shirts. It makes you wonder, "Man, where did all of that money go?" You have to spend time teaching your children both modesty and the value of the dollar.

Entertainment is another issue in which parents need to instruct their children. Movies, TV, magazines, and concerts today are totally off-the-wall. If you let your kid go to a concert, you have to be aware of what he listens to or watches on stage. Some groups are just pure filth. Even worse, these groups become role models because kids relate to the attitudes that are being communicated. Kids imitate their favorite groups—from their clothing to their philosophies. Personally, I believe that if you consistently allow your kids to go to these kinds of things, you are setting your child up for a fall. As they grow into adulthood, those images and songs will desensitize them to truth. Children imitate what they see and, unlike adults, they are unable to distinguish fantasy from reality.

When I was a little boy, about nine years old, I used to watch a show called *The Little Rascals*. In one episode, Alfalfa ate a bar of soap and when he talked bubbles came out of his mouth. It so much impressed my young mind that I went to the bathroom and took a big bite out of a bar of soap. I chewed it up, but no bubbles came out. The only bubble was my head. It was a sickening experience, but I did it because Alfalfa did it.

Kids do not always have a firm grip on reality. As a child I used to think that if I stepped off a cliff, I would hang there for a few seconds, realize that there was nothing holding me up, and then some how be able to run back to safety. Not only that, when my brothers and sisters were kids, we used to take the sheets off my parents' bed, stand on the roof, and jump, thinking the sheet was a parachute. Naturally, it was dangerous. But we imitated what we had seen. Whenever I watched something crazy, I would go try it. Now it is worse than ever because kids are watching shows with violent images that are inappropriate for adults, never mind children.

Even today's comic books can be dangerous because of their violent and graphic nature. A number of them have sexual artwork. It is our job to become aware of what is going on—it is at our kids' fingertips. Things that once were pure are now causing a callousness of heart and a loss of innocence in our youth.

Many TV programs are completely inappropriate for Christians to watch. Soap operas, sit-coms, and many of those so-called evening dramas are ungodly. Originally, soap operas were intended to sell soap. Now they sell dirt. Our job is to redeem our time. Not many TV shows draw you closer to the Lord. Mostly they desensitize you to sin. You would be wise to turn that junk off and occupy your time with something that pleases the Lord and edifies your soul.

PARENTS CAN BE CONTRIBUTORS

In Proverbs 30:11–12, the writer says:

> There is a generation that curses its father,
> And does not bless its mother.
> There is a generation that is pure in its own eyes,
> Yet is not washed from its filthiness.

We are living in that generation. Some of us can contribute to the problem because we have standards other than the Bible's. We watch shows or read things that are not godly, yet we tell our kids not to view or read those same things. God's priorities are lacking in our homes. Jesus said, "Do not labor for the food which perishes, but for the food which endures to everlasting life, which the Son of Man will give you, because God the Father has set His seal on Him" (John 6:27). The problem is that society is saying, "Labor for the meat that perishes—the more you have, the more you deserve. Take it, it is yours—even if it means sacrificing your family or your marriage. At least you'll be driving in style and looking good while you're doing it." Even Christians fall into this trap.

Maybe you never realized that raising a child would be this tough. You probably never anticipated the added expense. Had you realized that when the baby would cry at 2 AM your spouse would not always want to get up—and now you have to help? Before parenthood you had no idea these things existed. Remember when the two of you would go out on a Friday night and buy a few hamburgers. Now you buy twenty of them to feed a hungry family.

Have you noticed what kids do when you give them an allowance? They put it away. Then they come up to you at the store, saying, "Can I have a dollar, Dad?"

"What happened to your allowance?" you ask.

"I'm saving it."

They think they have two wallets: yours and theirs. You didn't expect this when you got married. When the baby was born, you imagined he would sleep all night, every night, for the rest of his life. Then one day he would wake up with a diploma in his hand, go off, and get married. You never conceived it was going to be this stressful.

Nevertheless, parenting is hard. Parents are not always right and often are not as sacrificial as they should be. Today, many parents are driven by guilt. They buy clothing, games, VCRs, and pay for parties in hopes of making their children feel valuable. Since "things" make them happy, they figure "things" will make their kids happy. But they are mistaken. Kids do not want things—they want a mother and a father. Material possessions can never replace the love and attention of a parent. Children need your time. And yet, time is scarce. You cannot run out and buy it. You have to sacrifice your own desires in order to give your children your time—it is death to self.

CHILDREN RULING THEMSELVES

The erosion of innocence is having its affect on our culture: children are dying, families are being destroyed, and society is crumbling. What some people may think is a step in the right direction, I say is an attack on our children and our society as a whole.

Isaiah once said, "As for My people, children are their oppressors, and women rule over them. O My people! Those who lead you cause you to err, and destroy the way of your paths" (Isaiah 3:12). Isn't this exactly what we are seeing today?

Because of broken homes and broken marriages, absentee parents and a lack of godly examples, many children are basically left alone to make critical decisions for themselves. Leaving children alone has contributed to a rise in rebellion, including the destruction of innocence that once went along with childhood.

In the book of Proverbs, we are warned about the results of failing to lead in our homes. The writer of Proverbs 29:15 says, "The rod and reproof give wisdom, but a child left to himself brings his mother to shame." Sadly, we are seeing this take place today. Children now rule in their homes. Children have become oppressors, and as they grow up without any kind of discipline, they bring shame to their families—ultimately, tearing our society apart.

When the Apostle Paul was writing prophetically concerning the last days, he wrote:

> But know this, that in the last days perilous
> times will come: For men will be lovers of

themselves, lovers of money, boasters, proud, blasphemers, disobedient to parents, unthankful, unholy, unloving, unforgiving, slanderers, without self-control, brutal, despisers of good, traitors, headstrong, haughty, lovers of pleasure rather than lovers of God, having a form of godliness but denying its power. And from such people turn away!

—2 Timothy 3:1–5

According to Paul, selfishness and materialism lead the list in the deterioration of a society.

This is exactly what we are witnessing today. People are lovers of money and lovers of self—lovers of their wishes, their plans, their desires—placing their own lives before their children's lives. If our desire for material gain comes before our families, then we create an environment that is not conducive to walking with Jesus. If we are not present within the home, training up our children, they are likely to become disobedient as Paul stated in his letter to Timothy. In the end, they will rebel against authority, no longer desiring to walk with Jesus Christ— they will have missed seeing the Christian life modeled for them by those who have the most influence in their lives, their parents.

Leading by Love

Love suffers long and is kind;

love does not envy;

love does not parade itself,

is not puffed up;

does not behave rudely,

does not seek its own,

is not provoked, thinks no evil;

does not rejoice in iniquity,

but rejoices in the truth;

bears all things,

believes all things,

hopes all things,

endures all things.

Love never fails.

—1 Corinthians 13:4–8

WALK IN LOVE

When you read this familiar passage of Scripture, it is revealing to put your own name in place of the word "love." *David* suffers long . . . Already I have to stop and admit that I do not exhibit patience as this verse indicates I should. Maybe if I were to really concentrate, I could make it through one day—maybe not. Well, if I could, then what about the other fifteen attributes of love that Paul lists in 1 Corinthians 13? Aside from Christ, no one can display all these qualities flawlessly. That is the point: we all fail—miserably. On our own, we cannot exemplify love towards our children, in the sense of biblical love. We need help. Actually, Jesus is the One who gives us hopeful news on this subject:

> And I will pray the Father and He will give you another Helper, that He may abide with you forever, even the Spirit of truth . . . for He dwells with you, and will be in you.
>
> —John 14:16–17

When Jesus left earth, He did not leave us alone. He left a deposit for all believers—the Holy Spirit. The Holy Spirit is our Helper, our Comforter. In all of life's undertakings, the Spirit is with the believer to help him accomplish God's purposes. And what better plan could our heavenly Father devise than parenting to mold us into the image of His Son?

To the Christian, there is no greater endeavor than parenting. With all the obstacles that society contributes, he would be helpless if it were not for the Spirit of God. As far back as the days of the early church, people were seeking solutions regarding parenting. Seeing their need, Paul addressed the heavy-hearted Ephesians, saying, "Walk in love, as Christ also has loved us" (Ephesians 5:2). Left to ourselves, we cannot meet this awesome requirement. The only way we can walk in this manner is if we continue down to verse eighteen, where Paul says, "But be filled with the Spirit."

To *walk in love*—to be godly parents, to sacrificially meet the needs of our families, to not raise our voices when the kids run across the carpets with muddy shoes—we need Spirit's empowering. We could never walk in this fashion ourselves. We lack holiness aside from the working of the Holy Spirit in us. Thus, we need to be filled with the Spirit. Before sharing any scriptural truths about raising children, I must say, "Abide in Christ." For you or I to live out our witness before our children, we have to be filled with the Spirit of God.

LEADING BY LOVE

God's Word instructs us to lead by love. Without the Spirit of God, emotions and humanistic advice often lead a parent's decision making. All you have to do is take a look at the world around you to realize that parents need wisdom. Though

countless numbers of books have been written on the subject—
and many of these are filled with godly advice—if the Holy
Spirit does not breath these truths into your life, then they are
mere words on a page.

After Paul addressed the Ephesians about their need to
walk in love and to *be filled with the Spirit,* he wrote these
words:

> Children, obey your parents in the Lord for this
> is right.
>
> "Honor your father and mother," which is the
> first commandment with promise: "that it may
> be well with you and you may live long on the
> earth." And you, fathers, do not provoke your
> children to wrath, but bring them up in the
> training and admonition of the Lord.
>
> —Ephesians 6:1–4

Notice, Paul addresses two groups of people: children
and fathers. Interestingly, he singles out fathers. Take note, too,
that Paul says, "Honor your *father* and mother. He does not say,
"Honor your *mother* and father." Obviously mothers are to be
honored as well as fathers. However, he puts fathers first and
addresses them twice in this passage, emphasizing a spiritual
order that needs to exist in the home.

Fathers are God's appointed spiritual leaders of the
home. Though much of the responsibility for training children is
shared with their wives; ultimately, fathers are responsible for
the spiritual climate in the home. A father's specific calling is to
be priest and provider for his family. This was the topic I chose
for a term paper when I was enrolled in a Marriage and Family

class. When I went to the university library, which had a tremendous volume of books, not a single book on a father's role in the home could be found. Perhaps things have changed over the last twenty years, but I think a father's role is often overlooked. In the world's eyes, bringing up children has largely been assumed to be a mother's role, and, for the most part, men have remained uninvolved. God's Word is not silent on this matter. He intends for fathers to have an active, vital role in bringing up their children.

THE PRIESTLY DUTIES

Fathers are God's appointed priests within the home. They do not have to be in public ministry, speak King James English, or wear a red-velvet robe. When the Bible uses the word *priest*, it refers to all Christians who have been called to represent God. His Word is planted in the hearts of believers so that they can minister to one another, stimulating one another to spiritual growth. A father's priestly duties include leading family worship, teaching the Word, and encouraging his children to have personal time with the Lord. Basically, he is to live out the Word of God before his family.

As "priest" describes a father's spiritual responsibilities, so "provider" describes his practical obligations. A father maintains faithful care and guidance for his family. He oversees the daily happenings of his children—his voice sounding warnings if they near danger, yielding advice if they need direction. He provides much more than the physical needs of his family; he administrates among all the members, maintaining the spiritual atmosphere in the home. Unfortunately, many fathers completely neglect their roles by leaving it to their wives.

In early Jewish culture a mother would train a child for the first year of a baby's life. As she nursed the child and provided for his physical needs, she talked about the Lord, sang spiritual songs, and encouraged the child in things of the Lord. Then, when the child had reached the age of two, the father took over by raising the child in spiritual and practical matters. He taught the children creedal statements and encouraged them to pray and memorize Scripture. These Hebrew fathers serve as role models for us. Fathers are to interact, teach, and lead their children in all spiritual matters. They are to be the spiritual authority in the home, not as a hard taskmaster but as a loving, gentle father.

FOLLOW AFTER JESUS

Maybe you recognize that you have failed to be that example of God's love to your family. I can certainly understand the pressures that Christian fathers go through. Together my wife and I have great concern for our four children—and we know our lives will impact them tremendously. Since God has called me also, as priest and provider to my family, I look to my Priest and Provider, Jesus Christ, for direction. In Mark 10:13–16, the author gives us insight into how Jesus dealt with children:

> They brought the young children to Him, that He might touch them; but the disciples rebuked those who brought them. But when Jesus saw it, He was greatly displeased and said to them, "Let

the little children come to Me, and do not forbid them; for of such is the kingdom of God. Assuredly, I say to you, whoever does not receive the kingdom of God as a little child will by no means enter it." And He took them up in His arms, put His hands on them, and blessed them.

First, notice that Jesus takes the children into His arms. He puts His hands on them and blesses them. Jesus' reaction to children was not like the disciples' reaction; He gladly welcomed them by embracing them. He even uses the opportunity to rebuke His disciples, teaching them that children are of great importance to God. And so, we learn that Jesus obviously desires children to come to Him. As a matter of fact, I would say that bringing children to the Lord Jesus Christ is of utmost importance. In Mark 9:42 Jesus said, "Whoever causes one of these little ones who believe in Me to stumble, it would be better for him if a millstone were hung around his neck, and he were thrown into the sea." Jesus makes it clear that bringing our children to Him—to a saving knowledge of the Lord Jesus Christ—should be our primary goal as parents.

Another obvious quality that both fathers and mothers can glean from Jesus is His affection. When the disciples tried to keep the children away from Jesus, He reached down, picked them up, and held them. Early on in my parenthood, I determined to be a touching father, a holding father. I wanted to be the kind of dad that was not afraid to show his affection, privately or publicly. As a youth I did not receive much physical affection, but when I became a new father I wanted to show my kids my love for them. *If Jesus is this way,* I had thought, *then I will be, too.* Demonstrating our love speaks volumes to young hearts.

God is committed to you and your children. He will give you everything you need to be a loving example to them. As you yield your life to the Spirit, He will work on your character. If you struggle with showing your love—demonstrating patience or kindness—He will make up for wherever you lack. There is no doubt you will make mistakes, but as you come to Him as a child of God, He will embrace you and help you.

If you have sin in your heart, confess it and leave it behind you (1 John 1:9). As you seek Him, read His Word and fellowship with His Spirit, you will begin to see changes in your life. You have an awesome calling—to impact your child's life as a priest. By His Spirit you can fulfill this duty, for it is "'Not by might, nor by power, but by My Spirit,' says the LORD of hosts" (Zechariah 4:6).

Lord, Please Train Me to Train My Child

Train up a child

in the way he should go,

and when he is old

he will not depart from it.

—Proverbs 22:6

TRAINING UP A CHILD

Lately popular public opinion has been for members of the community to train up children. People are looking to the church, the school, or some significant caretaker to educate their children. However, Proverbs 22:6 is not directed towards any of these individuals. Yes, children learn from direct interaction outside of the home; however, God's plan for the family is for moms and dads to train and protect their own children. No one else is going to care for and love a child the way that a parent does. Parents wield tremendous influence in the lives of their children. Therefore, it is vitally important that we do not relinquish our responsibilities to someone else. We have a call to "train up our children," and we need to heed that call.

Why then is there so little training happening in homes today? One reason may be that the word "training" carries with it negative connotations. Perhaps some people have not seen good parenting modeled for them. They may have been harshly disciplined themselves as children, and so, they see the role of a trainer as being controlling, or harsh. However, by neglecting to train a child, a parent is actually hindering that child from growing closer to the Lord. Never go overboard with punishment; yet, at the same time, realize that leniency produces hardness to correction, contributing to a lack of personal discipline in later life. Parents who mistakenly believe they are showing tenderheartedness to their children by not disciplining them are actually neglecting God's Word:

> And you, fathers, do not provoke your children to wrath, but bring them up in the training and admonition of the Lord.
>
> —Ephesians 6:4

Obviously, we are not to provoke our children to wrath (anger). The thought is to channel their spirits, not to destroy them. An overly restrictive parent can frustrate his child to the point where he no longer has influence in that child's life. This is not training in a biblical sense. Instead of being critical or cruel, which provokes a child to wrath, we are to train up our children by stirring up their spiritual appetites.

"Training up a child" is the same concept that a Hebrew midwife would use to nurse a newborn. A Hebrew midwife would pick up the newborn child, who had not yet learned how to nurse; and, taking a small portion, she would apply date-honey to the baby's lips. Tasting the sweetness of the honey, the infant would begin to move his mouth and tongue, provoking a sucking reflex. The child would quickly learn to nurse. In the same way, when you train up a child for the Lord, you need to provoke a reflex in the child's heart for things of the Lord. Our goal as parents is to provoke our children to nurse from the Word of God. This means that I need to love God myself. For as I love the Lord with all my heart, then I am nurturing within my children love for Him.

Before we can set goals and expectations for our children, we need to take a look at our own lives. The old adage is true: You cannot lead someone where you have not gone yourself. If we are ever to provoke our kids to righteousness, creating within them a hunger and thirst for God, we have to be hungering and thirsting after Him. It is more than having daily devotions—it is living out that devotion daily before your children. Let our prayer be, "Lord, please help my actions to match my words." Otherwise, we are setting ourselves up as hypocrites before our children.

We can probably all remember the coach who would say, "Go run two miles," but he had a tire around his middle. Remember thinking, *Why isn't he running with us*? More often than not, kids will respect their parents when they see them practice what they preach. Although at times instruction is verbal, most often our kids learn from what we do. There is a difference between teaching and training. Teaching imparts knowledge, whereas training develops the ability to do what is taught. Since we want our kids to have more than head knowledge about the Lord, our focus should be on developing skills within our children that match up to God's Word—and the way to accomplish this is by our example. If we want our kids to fear the Lord, we have to fear the Lord. If we tell our kids to show self-control, we need to show self-control. And if we tell our kids not to lie, but we take certain liberties to avoid the truth, we had better expect them to do the same. Our lives are mirrors of the Lord; our kids look to us to see what God's standards are. Of course, we will never be perfect, but we can ask the Lord to work in us so that we can be godly examples to our children. If we pray for this, surely He will answer our prayers.

In Ephesians, the apostle Paul instructs us to provoke our children in two ways: nurture and admonition. Nurturing is the training side of parenting. Really, it is the preventative role. Admonition, on the other hand, takes place after a child has broken the rules—it is the corrective side of parenting. Nurturing takes time, sacrifice, and consistency on the part of the parent. Admonishing takes a Spirit-filled parent who is both firm and loving. Both are necessary to bring up children and both we are commanded to do in Scripture.

As we nurture, we are preparing our children to make decisions for themselves. The goal is to see our children become independent, mature followers of Christ. Yet, nurturing is hard work. At times it will be exhausting, even frustrating. But by nurturing spiritual values within our kids, we help them avoid admonition, which can be unpleasant for everyone. Training requires effort and may be difficult for us to carry out, but the rewards far outweigh the cost. Actually, when parents nurture and admonish appropriately, they can trust that they are doing all that they can to accomplish their goal—to lead their children to Christ. Remember, you are not alone—the Lord will sustain you as you ask Him for strength and wisdom in training up your child.

IN THE WAY HE SHOULD GO

Proverbs 22:6 not only alerts us to the importance of training up a child, it recognizes the uniqueness of each child. "In the way he should go" means "in the child's way." Not every child is going to go the same way. Each child is wonderfully made (Psalm 139:14). Before I became a parent, I was quite knowledgeable about parenting—or so I thought. I believed that all children should be treated the same, thinking this would create stability and maintain fairness. Then I became a father. None of my theories worked. You see, at first I was extremely rigid. I did not understand that, like adults, all children are different; therefore, they have to be treated according to their God-given personalities. I had always placed the same expectations on them—all of my kids live by the same rules— but I have discovered that I have to treat them according to their personalities. For example, when my two sons were younger, one would respond if I simply told him that I was disappointed in him. Yet, his brother responded only to spankings. Both received the same training in terms of devotions, household rules, etc., but I had to treat them according to their individual personalities.

Although all four of my kids have very different personalities, I love each of them the same. If someone were to ask me, "Who is your favorite child?" I would respond, "The one sitting on my lap at the moment." I have never felt that one child was more precious than another—all four are very near to my heart. I make it a point that they know this. Once my son David thought that he would tease his older sister, Carin, so he said to her, "It's going to be neat when you move out. I think Dad would agree with me, too." When I came home Carin told me what he had said. "No," I told her, "I want you to be here with your mom and me. Even when you are gone and married, I want you to still feel that this is your home. There will always be a room for you, honey." Kids need to know that we want them. They need to know they are important to us.

One way we can communicate how important they are is by accepting them for who they are. God made them with their particular strengths and weaknesses, and we need to accept them completely. If a child is mechanically inclined but is pushed to be a scholar, he is not being encouraged to use the gifts that God has given him. Not all kids are going to be academic. My brother Frank is an example of this. He had a hard time learning how to read. As a matter of fact, I can still remember when he was eight years old and my mother had him read to her. As she held the book up, he read perfectly. There was only one problem. The pages were upside down. Instead of learning how to read the words on the page, Frank had memorized entire books that were read to him. He actually memorized them page-by-page. Maybe you have seen your kids do this. Their brains are incredibly sharp. They just memorize the pages like Frank had done. What he did excel at was auto mechanics. He could take an engine apart without a manual. He loved to work with his hands, and he was very good at it.

It is common for parents to worry over their child's development. Some parents may think, *How come my child is not reading as much as he should be?* Or, *Why is he always out in the garage tinkering with that old engine? He's just wasting his time out there.* But who knows what God is going to use your child to do. He may have the gift of working with his hands to help others. Here we are as parents trying to make our kids into preachers or doctors, when in reality He wants them to be airplane mechanics on the mission field. Rather than train our children to do what we think they are supposed to do, we should encourage them in the talents and gifts that God has given them.

In doing this, we are setting them free to be who they were created to be.

Not all children bring home straight *A*'s on their report cards. Some kids may work really hard just to pull off *C*'s. We will be wise if we recognize their abilities. If they bring home low scores, we should encourage them for doing the best they could do, if we know it is the best they could do. It's important for us to speak words of encouragement to our kids and help them to discover their natural gifts and abilities. It takes patience, time, and wisdom to understand your child. Observing and conversing with them is crucial. You will not discover who they really are until you do. Maybe your child has brought home a note from his teacher saying, "His work is messy," so you threaten him with punishment unless he improves. Then you tell him to pay better attention to his work. But how closely are you paying attention to him? Are you aware of what is going on inside his mind and spirit?

A long time ago I learned a very valuable lesson. The Lord showed me that little kids have bad days at school just as adults have bad days on the job. Your child might come home moody and grumpy because things have not gone well at school. Maybe she was called a name, or perhaps pushed down out on the playground. You may not be aware of it, but maybe she read poorly in front of the class. Often times we do not have a clear picture of what went on throughout our child's day. When she comes home with a poor attitude, we may want to discipline her on the spot. Perhaps we would scold, "Go to your room and come down when you can put on a happy face." Perhaps we should do some probing to find out why she is upset.

I can remember days when one of my kids would come home in a surly mood. Instead of disciplining, I would sit him down and start asking questions. "What's going on?" "What happened at school today?" For a lot of kids this is all it takes to open the line of communication open for you to reach inside and minister to them. "He shall die for lack of instruction, and in the greatness of his folly he shall go astray" (Proverbs 5:23). By not taking time to talk to our kids we are allowing them to suffer, which eventually causes them to go to outside influence for advice. Kids need their mothers and fathers to intervene when they are hurting. We need to direct them in how to deal with sad feelings and negative attitudes in a biblical manner. Often, they cannot do this on their own. Simply stated, they need us.

Playing favorites is another danger. This is the lesson recorded in the Bible about two brothers, Jacob and Essau. The Bible says that Isaac loved Essau; but Rachel loved Jacob. Competition and contention existed between the two brothers. It is a case of parents picking favorites. By choosing favorites, parents breed resentment and bitterness in their children. Bringing division into the home destroys families. Kids are extremely sensitive to whether they are being treated the same, for this is how they measure your love for them. We may not get along with a certain child as well as another, but we cannot let that stand in the way of our display of commitment to them. If we teach them that our Heavenly Father loves everybody the same, they will look to us to see if we are like Him.

WHEN HE IS OLD, HE WILL NOT DEPART FROM IT

The last part of Proverbs 22:6, "he will not depart from it," has often been misunderstood. Some people interpret it to mean that if they carefully follow Biblical guidelines their child's salvation is ensured. Unfortunately, we have no guarantees that our children will walk with the Lord. Scripture even records quite a few godly parents whose children did not walk with the Lord.

> *Adam and Eve* had a son named Cain. Cain killed his brother Abel.

> *Noah* had three sons, Shem, Ham, and Japheth. Ham shamed his father.

> The priest, *Eli*, had two sons who both were ungodly, Hophni and Phinehas.

> *David,* the sweetest psalmist of Israel, a man who was referred to in the Bible as "a man after God's own heart" had a son, Amnon, who raped his own sister. He also had a son named Absalom, who stole the hearts of the people of Israel from his own father.

> We know that *Solomon* had a son by the name of Jereboam, who actually was involved in the division of the nation of Israel.

> Then there was a godly king by the name of *Hezekiah*, who had a son whose name was Manasseh, one of the most evil kings Judah had ever seen.

Godly parents can raise ungodly children. We can do our best, but ultimately a child must make his own commitment to the Lord. Though we may carry a burden for a lost child, none of us can make an eternal decision for someone else. What we do have, however, is a command from God that we are to raise our children in the knowledge and fear of the Lord. We are to pass the torch of faith to our children.

We can teach our kids everything about life, but if we do not make every effort to pass on our faith, all of it is for nothing. If you think about it, we spend concentrated time teaching our kids a lot of things . . .

We teach them to walk and talk.

We teach them to be quiet and to sit still, to chew their food with their mouths closed, and not to speak with their mouths full.

We teach them to say "please" and "thank you."

We teach them important things like how to make sandwiches, how to pour milk without spilling it, how to blow their noses, to take baths, and to tie their shoes.

We teach them courtesy, trust, love, respect and patience for others (and sometimes yell at them when we are impatient).

We instruct them to look both ways when crossing the street and to play nicely by sharing their toys.

We teach them to not speak to strangers—but then we wonder why they are afraid to witness to people.

Have you given much consideration to what you are passing on to your kids? Much of our time is used in developing life skills that they will need. They need to learn to tie their shoes and to share, yet of all the important messages to get across faith in Jesus needs to be top priority. If we are willing to spend so much time on temporal matters, how much more effort should we concentrate in communicating about eternity?

We may think that we communicate with our children clearly, but we may be sending mixed messages. Our actions and reactions can undermine the lessons we try to develop in our children if we are not careful. To instruct them in having patience and respect we should display patience and respect them as individuals, being careful not to yell at them when they make mistakes or when they are disobedient. If we teach them not to talk to strangers, we must consider whether we are limiting their boldness. There is wisdom in communicating, and as we seek the Lord, He will instruct us so we can instruct our children.

Training them up in things of the Lord has got to be our life's ministry. We cannot let anything stand between our kids and the Lord. We need to nurture within them a love and desire for Him. We can do this by relating with each one individually just as God relates with each of us individually. When all is said and done, our hope is that they will have picked up the torch of faith which we have placed before them.

Obedience Comes
From Love

If you keep My commandments, you will remain
in My love, just as I have my Father's commands
and remain in His love.

—John 15:10

Obedience is from the heart of God. In every generation we see evidence of this. Back when the Israelites wandered the wilderness, God made a way for them to enter the Promised Land, but their leader would not be heading up that journey. God gave the task to Joshua, who was second in command, because Moses had failed to properly represent God to His people. Israel's father figure disobeyed the Lord. Moses was no worse a sinner than the rest of us, but God removed his blessing because of his act of disobedience. If the Lord takes obedience this seriously, so should we.

In light of this, Joshua delivered these words to the Israelites:

> And if it seems evil to you to serve the LORD, choose for yourselves this day whom you will serve, whether the gods which your fathers served that were on the other side of the River, or the gods of the Amorites, in whose land you dwell. But as for me and my house, we will serve the LORD.
>
> —Joshua 24:15

This call to commitment is just as much for us today as it was for God's people when Joshua delivered it. It is up to you to make the choice. Will you choose to serve the gods of the land in which you dwell, or the true and living God?

As leader of your home, you have the same responsibility Joshua had—you are the model of obedience to your family. Notice, Joshua made the decision to serve the Lord for himself and his family. Have you made such a declaration to both the Lord and your family? In order to lead, we have to let our children know that we have given them to the Lord. Our faith cannot be silent. Lately it has become popular to say, "I am giving my kids liberty to make their own decisions. They can choose to serve the Lord on their own." Well, if Joshua had been that kind of leader, the people would not have followed him into the Promised Land. People need strong leaders. From the top level of a society down to the intimate setting of the family, God places leaders over people to maintain His purposes. This is why it is so important that we obey our leaders. God has put people in headship over us, and as we are submitting to them, we submit to God.

GOD'S PLAN FOR THE FAMILY

In the book of Ephesians, Paul points out that obedience comes from a twofold relationship: children are required to obey their parents; and parents are required not to provoke their children to wrath. Our children have a responsibility to be obedient to us, and we have a responsibility to not violate that relationship. We should never abuse or misuse our children in any way, shape, or form. The Lord has given us authority over our children to guide, protect, and develop within them a love for things of the Lord. The family is the training ground where a child learns how to obey his parents, ultimately learning to obey the Lord.

It should be of no surprise that Paul gives children a command to obey their parents—it does not just come naturally. Maybe you have heard some parents claim, "Oh, she is just a compliant child." Some children have stronger wills than others do, but one thing is certain, we all are born with a sin nature. Proverbs 22:15 states, "Foolishness is bound up in the heart of a child." In each of us there lies a natural propensity toward rebellion—just something in our nature that causes us to rebel. You know this by getting on the freeway. People get behind the wheel and the fleshly nature takes over. But when we look at a tender infant we think, "How innocent she looks." When, in fact, underneath that sweet smile is a sinner just like you and me. We all have sinned, and we all fall short of the glory of God (Romans 3:23).

Children need to be taught at a young age to put to death their fleshly nature. By teaching them early in their lives to submit to the Lord, you are developing a habit that will last a lifetime. What greater lesson can we teach our kids? Each young life needs to be directed in how to submit his heart to the Lord. And it does not happen overnight. It takes time, sacrifice, and re-education along the way.

KEYING INTO WHAT IS IMPORTANT

Unfortunately, many parents are on a treadmill. They are off chasing illusions. As a result, many parents become driven by guilt. Feeling badly, uninvolved parents tend to give their children things rather than time and attention. People are too busy to make time for their children. In fact, I was looking at the newspaper—I think it was Dear Abby's column—and I read a story about a little boy who was asked by his Momma, "What do you want for Christmas?" Do you know what he said? "Time." Many parents would just as soon give him a VCR or a bike rather than time. "I always wanted a bike when I was growing up," they will say. In actuality they are giving their kid a bike so they can have a break. Plenty of people do it. Pretty soon this lack of involvement is going to stir up resentment and anger, ultimately resulting in disobedience to parents and to the Lord.

One of the most heart-piercing stories recorded in the Bible is found in the book of Genesis. In the twenty-second chapter we find the account of a father's total obedience. Abraham was called upon by God to sacrifice his only son, Isaac. More than Abraham's only son, Isaac was his long-awaited son—some twenty-five years. Could it be that God asked this loving father to put his son to death? Why would a God of compassion and mercy have a father take the life of his own son?" The answer is simple: Obedience. God wanted to test the faith of a father, and set a precedent for all fathers who followed him. A great lesson lies in Abraham's willingness to put to death his life-long dream. By obeying God, Abraham pleased His Father and taught his son a valuable lesson: God is faithful to His promises.

WE MUST DIE TO SELF

The bittersweet lessons of obedience are unavoidable. The screaming, the crying, the constant questioning "why" begins to wear you down. The infant spits his food out all over you because he doesn't like the spinach you just fed him. The stubborn teen rolls his eyes or averts your gaze to challenge your authority. Parenting takes continued dying to the fleshly nature. At times, we want to rebel just as much as our kids do. We may even answer our children in sharp tones because they use them with us. But God is dealing with us as much as He is dealing with our kids. By testing our patience and proving our character, He refines us into vessels of honor. Once yielded, we are usable tools in the Lord's hand to mold the hearts of our children. God begins the heart-shaping lesson of obedience in us first, so that we will lead by our godly example.

It is so important to explain over and over what we expect from our kids. Repetition is one of the most draining aspects of parenting, yet so necessary. It would be a lot easier if we could just sit a child down at a young age and say, "Honey, the Lord loves you, and the way that you can love Him back is by always obeying me." Imagine, he then looks into your eyes adoringly and responds, "Yes, Daddy." Instant obedience. Can you imagine it being that easy? But this is not God's design. The Lord uses the constant challenges we experience with our kids to work His love into our hearts. It is because He is patient with us, we in turn should be patient and gracious with them. We may repeat the same lesson for months, even years, but our message must be clear: obeying the Lord is the best thing to do.

Kids are observant. They catch on to what they *see* much more than to what is *said* to them—even if you repeat yourself ten times. Toddlers are a good example. They mimic everything you do. They like to make the same faces daddy makes, and pretend to stir dinner along with mommy in the kitchen. Then, for some reason, as they grow older we expect them to learn strictly by listening, not realizing that they still learn by observation. Of course, older children should be more accountable for what they are told, but they still need strong role models in their lives. If you take a look at Jesus' teaching style, you will quickly find that He did not speak out everything He wanted to communicate. He taught by example. The best teachers do. So if we want our kids to graduate from the school of obedience, we need to become doing and being teachers, not just saying teachers.

OBEDIENCE COMES FROM LOVE

Displaying love and acceptance makes it easier for children to obey. I did not say easy, I said easier. If your child dislikes what you have told her, but your love and support back it up, she will learn to submit out of love and respect. Yelling and threatening undermine your authority. Think about your relationship with God. Because of His great love for you, you love Him back—and you prove your love to Him by being obedient to Him. The same is true with our kids. Our unconditional love for them should stir them to obey.

Showing love does not mean saying yes to everything. You need to offer patient guidance and continue to let your children know who is in control. If you are too harsh, you can jeopardize their trust. But if you are too easy, they will not listen to you or respect you. So our prayers need to be for wisdom and discernment. When you come to the end of your patience, ask the Lord to fill you with His Spirit, enabling you to do what you cannot do on your own. At times like these, I go to the Word of

God and look for Scripture to enlighten me on what I am supposed to do.

Obedience comes by practice, so forming godly habits needs to start early. From the time a child is born, we have to seek to place God's truth in his heart. We need to teach him that obeying God's Word is of utmost importance. If we let things slip, thinking, "Oh, he's really cute—he's too young to understand what he is doing," then we are setting him up for failure down the road. Children can understand truth at a very young age. And so, by teaching them what God values early on, they will develop respect for what is important to Him. If we give our children too much freedom and then try to take it away from them later, they will rebel—not just against us but against the Lord, too.

When my kids make wrong choices, I see it as an opportunity to instruct them in the things of the Lord. I try not to react with surprise or disappointment because if I do, it will affect how they receive what I have to say to them. Thus, I seek to take care of disobedience right away. If we fail to correct our children, we fail to train them to obey the Lord. For instance, if your child back talks you; but you are too tired to deal with it, then you are failing to mold and shape his heart and mind to fear the Lord. Love does what is needed at the moment, no matter how tired.

WHAT ARE YOU GIVING YOUR CHILD?

"What values am I nurturing in my child?" This question should constantly be on our minds. We cannot be ignorant about how our values are transferred. If we spend extra time at work, laboring for material wealth, our children will learn that material things are important. We may tell them that spiritual matters come first, but they learn the truth by observing our lives. To influence your child to accept godly values, you will have to live out those values before him day in and day out. You cannot merely declare that something is important; you have to prove it by your actions. Values are caught rather than taught.

It is important for us to be in tune with the Spirit of God. If we walk in the Spirit, our kids will learn what it looks like to be close to the Lord. But if we walk according to our flesh, we are training them to respond with actions that are not fitting for a Christian. I do not say these things to discourage you if you have been making mistakes. We all make mistakes. I am thankful that God is forgiving and He restores us. He gives us "beauty for ashes, the oil of joy for mourning, and the garment of praise for the spirit of heaviness" (Isaiah 61:3). Each day is a new day. If your values have not been what they should be, God will forgive you—you can start afresh because His mercies are new every morning.

It is absolutely needful for us to adopt kingdom-of-God values, not worldly values. We have to present values that are good, noble, and strong—modeling Biblical values to our children. Think about the cartoons that are popular today. What values do they teach? Disobedience is one. Material wealth is another. The Bible teaches a man's life does not consist of his possessions. Principles shape our values. If we value material wealth, our kids will, too. Kids pick up on values very early in life, and if we do not show them that the Lord is the Owner of all that we have, then they will value all that we have instead of Him. Values will either draw a person closer to Jesus Christ, making him or her into an obedient child of God; or values can turn someone away from Him to seek after his own desires.

Unfortunately, parents who have sought to transfer their faith to their children do not always succeed. The only guarantee we have in life is that Jesus Christ died for our sins. And each of us has to receive that gift for ourselves. Even if we have kept a steady walk with the Lord, living it out honestly and sincerely before our kids, they can still choose to rebel. The only thing that you and I are called to do is train up our children in the Lord. The rest is left up to your child and the working of the Holy Spirit in his or her life. I might add, we have to be very careful not to become Job's comforters toward parents with prodigal sons and daughters. It cannot be assumed that a parent is responsible for a child who is in rebellion. In times like these, we need to give each other support and bear one another's burdens. The best that any of us can do is to love the Lord and trust Him with the souls of our children.

Love Disciplines

For whom the LORD loves He disciplines, just as a father the son in whom he delights.

—Proverbs 3:12

Certain traits I see in my children I know they received from me. When my son David was about three years old, we had to punish him for something he had done wrong. "You know, Son," I had said, "You are going to need to go to your room." So he was sent to his room to think about what he had done—supposedly. How much can a three-year-old really think? Not long after I heard some noises. *Better check this out,* I had thought. So up to his room I went, only to walk in and see David jumping up and down on his bunk bed, smashing his head on the ceiling. Cherry red in the face, he continued bouncing up and down as he beat himself up. *Oh, no!* I remember thinking, *He's just like me.*

You see, I used to do that, too. When my brother and I were little, my mother would send us to our room as a form of punishment. It all started one day after we both had been sent to our room, which we shared. My brother, Frankie, had said, "Hey, let's make Mom feel bad. Let's hit our heads on the wall." So we did. I can remember just banging my head on the wall, thinking all the time that I was punishing Mom by giving myself a bump on the forehead. Most likely you can imagine what she did. From all the noise, she started towards our room to come and check on us. Frankie and I could hear her footsteps as she neared our room, which encouraged us to bang even harder.

Then the door opened. Mom walked in, saw what we were up to, and remarked, "Make sure you don't damage that wall." Promptly turning around, she walked out of the room and left us to our game, closing the door behind her.

So when I found my little David jumping up and down on his bed for all he was worth, trying to inflict pain on himself and on me, I thought, *Oh, Lord, please help me. I know what's going to happen in a few years—he's going to be just like me.* The Lord reminded me of what my mother had done, so I said, "Make sure you don't put a hole in that wall." And after I had walked out into the hall he stopped.

Moments will arise when we will need immediate discernment in how to discipline our kids. Maybe we will be able to reflect on a past experience—a time when something really worked with our kids. Sometimes we will heed the advice that comes from another parent. Or it could be that we would need to call upon the Lord, asking Him to show us what to do. Whatever the case, discipline is going to be costly. It is going to require our finest judgment, our patience, and our submission to the Lord so that we can make wise decisions.

DECIDING TO DISCIPLINE

Even before we step into the dark corridor of discipline, we need to determine whether we should go there or not. There will be times when our kids will just be kids—they are young and sometimes foolish. I do not believe that we should discipline childishness that is not outright rebellion. Maybe a bouncy toddler needs to be redirected, or an energetic youth sent outside to run around. Over the years, I have come to realize that not every careless act is deserving of correction or criticism. Sometimes kids just need to be listened to or refocused. Only a parent can make the call. But we should never discipline a child for failing to do something that he or she is not capable of doing. Before we step in to correct a child's behavior, we need to ask ourselves, "Is this something that he or she can handle?" When the remote control is left out within the grasp of a baby, it is not reasonable to expect him to stay away from it—that is more than the baby can handle at that point. Discipline should be saved for instances when kids have clearly broken the rules and can be held accountable for their behavior. So we need to have wisdom as to whether our child is just being childish, or whether he really requires the "rod of discipline."

Realizing your child's abilities should come into play before you make a judgment against them. For instance, many times a small child does not realize he is lying. Under the age of eight years old, children have not reached complete moral development. Young children may see their answers as means to appropriate something that they want—they may not exactly understand what a lie is. Generally, between the ages of eight and ten years old, children begin to develop moral character. And by the time they are twelve years old, they are pretty knowledgeable about moral expectations. Regardless of a child's age, parents still need to teach their child the difference between right and wrong; realizing the child's maturity level helps in knowing how to deal with him.

THE PURPOSE OF DISCIPLINE

Hebrews 12:10 says, "For they indeed . . . chastened us as seemed best to them, but He for our profit, that we may be partakers of His holiness." Contrary to our natural understanding, discipline is meant to bring a blessing. Its goal is to bring God's people to a kind of maturity where obedience is the rule, rather than the exception. Its focus is to turn us from our sin, bringing us back into fellowship with God. When we discipline our kids, we need to keep in mind the Lord's purposes. Restoring our children into fellowship with God and with others is the greatest lesson we can teach them.

God's discipline is perfect. His work in our lives is to chastise us, not to punish us. Even though these words are often used interchangeably, they differ greatly in their meanings. Punishment is the work of a judge, casting judgment and upholding the law; chastisement, however, is the work of a father, for it is born out of love. Our loving Father works in our lives to make us more into the image of His Son. He does not become angry when He corrects us. And He is not looking to inflict pain upon us. The opposite is true. He wants us to have His very best. He wants it so much that He is willing to let us suffer a little through correction so we might share in the peaceable fruit of righteousness. Children need to recognize that negative behavior causes negative results. Thus, our disciplining should bring a fear in doing wrong. And so, our duty as Christian parents is to discipline our children as God disciplines His children. This involves affirmation, correction, criticism, praise, and rebuke. Depending on the need that arises, any one of these five may be necessary—maybe all five.

GRACE OR CHASTISEMENT?

When I reach a fork-in-the-road along the path of parental decision-making, I ask God to give me wisdom and discernment. At this point, I stop and pray, "Which path should I take, Lord? Grace or chastisement?" As we seek the Lord for guidance, we can trust that He will tell us which way to go. "Your ears shall hear a word behind you, saying, 'This is the way; walk in it,' whenever you turn to the right hand, or whenever you turn to the left" (Isaiah 30:21). Now, we will never be perfect; but if our hearts are submitted to the Lord, we are starting off from a good position. If we mess up, we have only to go back to God to seek Him again. But if we do not start off by asking Him, we are sure to take lots of dead-end routes, which will leave us exasperated and feeling helpless. I recommend that you wait to start any course of action before consulting the Lord. He is faithful to direct us to the right route concerning our children.

When David was a young boy, I wanted to teach him the difference between grace and chastisement. One day he was really acting up, so I said, "Son, you know what you've done is wrong, so I'm going to spank you." He began to cry out, "Grace! Grace! Grace!" *He understands,* I thought. You see, a few days before he had misbehaved, so I had said to him, "Son, I really ought to spank you, but I'm not going to. Understand, Son, you deserve to be spanked for what you did, but I want you to learn the meaning of the word "grace." God gives us grace when He doesn't punish us—and you deserve to be punished." A few days later, he acted up again. This time I said, "You know, Son, I am going to spank you." By his response I could tell that he understood our discussion from the other day. Even though he cried for grace, this time it was evident that he needed punishment. "No," I told him, "Today it's the law." That time he got his spanking.

DISCIPLINE IS AN ACT OF LOVE

If we fail to seek the Lord by daily reading His Word, we will not discipline our kids the way that we should. We need to be empowered by the Spirit so that we act out of love and not from our flesh. We have to be aware of the fact that we are in a battle. The problem is a lot of parents have not realized that they have to discipline kids to deal with their human nature. Folly is bound up in the heart of a child. Even secular observers would agree to this.

An excerpt taken from the Minnesota Crime Commission states, "Every baby starts life as a little savage. He is completely selfish and self-centered. He wants what he wants, when he wants it—his bottle, his mother's attention, his playmate's toys. Deny him these and he seethes with rage and aggressiveness, which would be murderous were he not so helpless . . . This means that all children are born delinquent— not just certain children, but all children. If permitted to continue in their self-centered world of infancy, given free reign to their impulsive actions to satisfy each want, every child would grow up a criminal, a thief, a killer, a rapist."

Notice this excerpt does not come from a Christian organization—it is secular. The bottom line is that children are born with an evil human nature.

Thus, without concentrated effort and prayerful guidance, a child will go his own way. The result will be destruction. The writer of Proverbs 14:12 says, "There is a way which seems right to a man, but its end is the way of death." This is true for our children, too. If we allow a child to go his own way, he ultimately will do something that brings his own destruction. As we discipline our children, we need to recognize that we are grabbing them out of the reaches of hell, out of eternal destruction.

Discipline is an act of love and when we discipline our kids they should know this. A parent who is harsh and yells a lot is really doing more damage than good. If discipline is to change your child's heart, then he needs to know that it is being done from a heart that deeply loves him—that is deeply committed to him. We know this is true from the following passage in Hebrews:

> And you have forgotten the exhortation which speaks to you as to sons:
>
> *"My son, do not despise the chastening of the LORD, nor be discouraged when you are rebuked by Him; for whom the LORD loves He chastens, and scourges every son whom He receives."*
>
> If you endure chastening, God deals with you as with sons; for what son is there whom a father does not chasten? But if you are without chastening, of which all have become partakers, then you are illegitimate and not sons. Furthermore, we have had human fathers who corrected us, and we paid them respect. Shall we not much more readily be in subjection to the Father of spirits and live? For they indeed for a few days chastened us as seemed best to them,

but He for our profit, that we may be partakers
of His holiness. Now no chastening seems to be
joyful for the present, but grievous; nevertheless,
afterward it yields the peaceable fruit of
righteousness to those who have been trained by
it.

—Hebrews 12:5–11

There is really no way to get around it: discipline is
painful. It hurts our kids and it hurts us. So it is in everyone's
best interest to avoid discipline by consistently training our
children. Through consistent training, we are giving them the
tools to make mature, godly decisions—hopefully enabling them
to escape discipline's sting. Inevitably, at times they will need
the pain of chastisement to catch their attention and put them
back on the right path. Even though it is not pleasant, each act of
correction or chastisement works to mold your child into the
person he or she will become. Thus, if we neglect this
undesirable duty, we are neglecting our child. They definitely do
not want it, but it is certainly what they need. Every wise mother
and father disciplines their child because, in doing so, they are
looking out for their child's best interest—to be nearer to God.

CHOOSING THE CONSEQUENCES

Once we decide to chastise our child, we need to choose which
action best fits the situation. Really, I think circumstances and
behaviors—the events that lead up to your decision to
discipline—will dictate the consequences. Also, it will depend
largely on their ages and temperaments. As I have mentioned
before, I have dealt with my four kids very differently based on

their unique personalities. For some children, a spanking may be appropriate—it will modify their behavior. Yet, for others, corporal punishment may not be the best form of discipline. Some kids respond to a stern look or a serious voice better than they would to a spanking. Each child is different, so we need to find the best way to deal with one according to his unique makeup.

I have never had to spank my son, Joseph, or my daughter, Anna. I have always been able to discuss issues with them and they have listened to me. All I really had to do was tell them that they disappointed me or they made a mistake. Their behavior was modified because of their love for their mom and me. On the other hand, when David was little it was a completely different story. Both he and his sister, Carin, have strong personalities. Carin is my actress. I can remember raising my hand to spank her when she was little, and before I could finish, she was screaming, "Child abuse!" Apparently, she had heard that term used at school. I am sure at times our neighbors wondered what was happening at our house. Of course, her over-reacting made it even more difficult. So over the years I have had to learn how to deal with each of my children on an individual level. Experience by experience, you will learn to determine what is best for your child, especially as you rely on the Lord to direct you.

THREE THINGS TO BE

There are three things that I always keep in mind when I discipline my kids. First, *be consistent.* If you say to your child, "Daddy is going to spank you on the count of three," and then, after counting to three, you continue to reason with the child, then you are teaching him that you do not mean what you say. It is subtle, but it is true.

Secondly, *be quick*. Long delays between the discipline and the behavior send the wrong message. We want to teach our kids to quickly repent and deal with their sin. By quickly punishing them so it is over and done with, they can learn that God quickly forgives them and remembers their sin no more.

Thirdly, *be fair*—let the penalty fit the crime. I hear stories of kids who are either let off the hook when chastisement is needed, or who are given extremely harsh sentences for very minor infractions. Neither of these are God's way to discipline. Yes, we need to be gracious and teach them about the Lord's character; however, by letting them off the hook too often, we are not emphasizing the holiness of God and the need to revere His Word and His ways. Then again, by punishing them too severely, we are not accurately representing our Heavenly Father. He is not harsh in His treatment of us. His purpose is for us to know Him and love Him more deeply.

By being consistent, being quick to address the issue, and by executing wisdom in our judgements we will better represent the Lord to our children.

THE IMPORTANCE OF COMMUNICATION

Communication is probably the most important part of discipline. You need to talk through why you are punishing your child and what expectations you have for him or her. Young children especially need to have values explained to them—even repeated over and over—for through our explanation, we are ingraining in them God's ways. Older children benefit from communication just as much. However, they need to be listened to more, and directed less—they need to see that what they have to say really matters, and if their thinking is wrong, we can take the opportunity to present them with the truth.

Another goal of communication is to teach our children the importance of reconciliation. Kids need to recognize their sin and be given the opportunity to repent of it. A typical scenario in our house would go something like this. . . After sending a child to his room, I'd come in and ask, "Why were you in your room?" And if he would respond, "I don't know," which he often did, I would say, "Oh, yes, you do." We would further discuss what he had done, leading him to realize his need to confess his sin. Once he had identified what he had done wrong, then I would urge him to ask for forgiveness, although it may not always happen immediately. I think all families will have their share of this kind of struggle. But really, we should view these opportunities as teachable moments—living sermons about the Lord and His ways.

As you communicate with your kids, let them know that you trust them. Coming from a biblical perspective that love believes all things (1 Corinthians 13:8), I have a tendency to give my kids the benefit of the doubt. On occasion, when I find that one of my kids is not being truthful with my wife or me, then I sit them down to discuss it. I explain to them that truth is essential—that it is the foundation of every relationship. I also let them know that there are consequences for lying or being deceptive. Normally, I will say, "I'm giving you a chance to come clean." And, overwhelmingly, they would respond to this kind of dialogue by seeking repentance, if they were guilty. Even if they lie to me, I know that the Lord will deal with them. Ultimately, I believe that trust is the best thing to use in dealing with children—for trust is a tool to open their hearts.

One of the hardest and most significant lessons we can instill in our children is to respect authority. If you have a teenager in the house, you have most likely experienced a challenge to your authority. Exodus 20 states that a child is to respect his mother and father. Yet, more and more, we are seeing an utter lack of respect in our kids—even in Christian households. The battle for power started back in the Garden of Eden and it has not gone away since sin's inception—disrespect is a vital tool of the enemy. That is why we need to insist on respect from our children. Any time one of my children talks back to Marie or me, I immediately respond, "You need to stop that right now." Disrespect cannot be tolerated. By being firm and letting them know the seriousness of their offense. We are teaching them to have self-control over their emotions. Likewise, we need to keep our feelings intact as we deal with them. Parents who are respected by their kids are often those parents who esteem God's Word. We are admonished in the book of Ephesians to "not provoke" our children to wrath. Using belittling language or refusing to hear your child out will shut down all communication between the two of you. Remember you are their best model of how to handle conflict. If you want them to learn how to deal with issues in a godly manner, you are their best teacher.

After disciplining, we need to extend reassurance to our kids. They need to see that we have forgiven them and that we will not bring up the matter again—which may be difficult to do.

Psalm 103:12 says, "As far as the east is from the west, so far has He removed our transgressions from us." They need to see that by dealing with their sin before God, they are forgiven and restored back into fellowship. When they have sought out forgiveness, then the incident is over. God treats us this way, so we need to extend such grace and mercy to our children.

James 1:5 says, "If any of you lacks wisdom, let him ask of God, who gives to all liberally and without reproach, and it will be given to him." Do you lack wisdom in dealing with your child? God knows exactly what he or she needs. Seek Him. Prayer is your greatest tool. He will lead you by His Spirit as you faithfully discipline your child.

Becoming an Influence

Hold fast the pattern of sound words which you have heard from me, in faith and love which are in Christ Jesus.

—2 Timothy 1:13

I was talking to my daughter just the other day and my eyes welled with tears. "I just don't have much longer for you to be in the house," I said. "You are growing older and someday soon you are going to be out of the house." It was a moment that touched me deeply, bringing realization that this stage in our relationship was drawing to a close.

The day will come when your little ones will be ready to leave you, and at that time you will reflect upon the impact that you have made in their lives. I am nearing that time now, and I have already begun to think about it. *What kind of effect have I had on them? What have I done to encourage them to love and serve Jesus?* I may never clearly know the answers to questions like these. Parenting truly is a journey of faith. Along the way, the Spirit guides you; but ultimately, God is in control. Each day that you have spent with your child and every word that you have spoken have been woven together into the fabric of his life. And although the training, disciplining, and nurturing will come to an end, you will always be an influence. I think that this really hit me when I read David's words to his son, Solomon, as his life neared its end:

Then the days of David drew near that he should die, and he charged Solomon his son, saying: "I go the way of all the earth; be strong, therefore, and prove yourself a man. And keep the charge of the LORD your God: to walk in His ways, to keep His statutes, His commandments, His judgments, and His testimonies, as it is written in the law of Moses, that you may prosper in all that you do and wherever you turn; that the LORD may fulfill His word which He spoke concerning me, saying, 'If your sons take heed to their way, to walk before Me in truth with all their heart and with all their soul,' He said, 'you shall not lack a man on the throne of Israel.'"

—1 Kings 2:1–4

CALLED TO INFLUENCE

Notice, even as David was about to die, he had one commission: to continue to minister to his son, Solomon, who would soon be king. David lived like I want to live—He blessed his family to the very end. His influence lasted his entire lifetime.

I have come to realize that my influence will be for a lifetime, too. You see, you do not quit being a father when your kids move out or get married. This may be the attitude of some people, but this viewpoint is supported nowhere in Scripture. That is why I find David's story so instructive. I see the commitment of David to his son, even as he lies on his deathbed. He is acting out his priestly role within the home by instructing his beloved son, Solomon. David knew that a father never ceases being a father, and thus, even though he was speaking to his adult son, he spoke as father to son. David's example has inspired me to take up the same commission he did—to be an influential father as long as I live.

GROWING PAINS

In life we each go through stages and when you have children, you will experience growing pains together. As your children grow up, in a sense, you grow right along with them. Each stage that they enter is new for them, but it is also new for you. As my kids have each reached their teens, I have had to learn to relate with them differently. In the earlier years of their lives, I acted as a disciplinarian, which was necessary to train them for adulthood. But as they have moved into young adulthood they have needed more freedom to make their own decisions—to grow up. At this point, you need to relate from a position of influence rather than solely from a position of authority. They are struggling to mature; you are struggling to release control. You will escape a lot of heartache by recognizing that this is a necessary phase for your teen, and that this season will come to an end. It is just a part of the parenting process.

For most parents, this transition in their child's life is a challenge. Conflicts arise when their opinions differ radically from yours. You may think this is pure rebellion, but it is not necessarily rebellion just because your child disagrees with you. In order for them to become a young adult who owns their ideas and learns to express their opinions, they will disagree with you. It is unwise to enter into arguments. Certainly, I am not saying that blatant disrespect should go undisciplined. We have a responsibility to correct them until they are full-grown mature believers. Often the tension you are experiencing with your child is just their attempt to become an adult. These growing pains signal that the relationship is nearing a time when you will hand over your position of authority in your child's life. During this stage, the best thing to do is seek the Lord, asking Him what part you are to play during these particularly uncomfortable times.

Teens desire to be seen as responsible individuals. Because of this it may seem as if your child is cutting you off, but most likely this is not the case. Your teenager is expressing his need to become an adult—he wants your trust and respect. Now, of course, he may not be living as responsibly as you want him to, but he is really crying out for your approval and your love. Love him unconditionally through this season. Remind him to pray and seek the Lord in his decisions. Be especially sensitive and available to listen to him when he opens up to talk to you. The Lord will mature your faith and your prayer life as you seek Him for answers concerning your teenager.

GAINING GROUND

God has given us the responsibility to be overseers, which means that we do not have a license to run our children's lives. If I do not like a decision my son or daughter makes, I have to know when to let go and when to speak out. Even if experience allows me to see down the road and I know they are setting themselves up for a fall, I need to let my child make his or her own mistakes. Hopefully, I will have established a good enough relationship with him that when he does fall down he will feel free to come to me and speak with me about it.

Now, it is not always easy to put up with some of the things that your teenager may say or do during this metamorphosis. Keep in mind, sometimes kids say things for shock value. For example, when my son, David, was thirteen years old he got angry and said, "I don't believe in the God that you teach about. I'm not a Christian!" Knowing how important this is to me, he said this to inflict pain on me when his temper had flared. At times like these, we need to know how to respond to our child in grace. If chastisement is appropriate for ungodly attitudes or speech, then we need to exercise our authority. However, we may not always react appropriately either. We may react to a comment in our flesh, not being led by the Spirit. If this is the case, we need to pray for the Spirit to give us self-control.

Also, we need to learn to weigh our children's comments. Consider who they are as a person. Whom do you know them to be when they are not angry or in a bad mood? Listen to them and try to respect their opinions, even if you disagree with them. Treat them according to who they are in Christ. No, I am not suggesting that we compromise the truth; I am suggesting that we ask for the Lord to reveal His truth to us so we can treat our children accordingly. With the Lord's help, doing these things has greatly helped me in knowing how to respond to my children.

Some parents strive to become best friends with their kids as they near adulthood in an attempt to relate with their young-adult child. This fosters an unhealthy relationship. A parent is never truly a friend to a child, though we can act in the role of a friend. The parent's age and experience mitigate against a genuine friendship in the sense that you would have with another person of the same sex and the same age. I do not discount the sentiment involved—I believe there should be friendly conversations. Mothers and daughters, fathers and sons, should spend time together in activities that they enjoy, but they need to maintain their roles. Their roles are different.

Respecting the role that God has given you with your child will pave the way for you to influence him more than if you were his friend. I enjoy a warm, friendly relationship with my children, but I do not expect them to treat me as they treat their friends. The problem occurs when the need for authority arises. Somebody has to make a decision and if there is no authority between you two because you are friends, then there is a problem. You cannot be a parent on one day and a buddy and friend the next. Parents should understand who they are in respect to their children, and vice-a-versa. This does not stifle your influence in your child's life. In fact, I believe it gives you greater influence. Children look for role models to emulate; they need us to be a loving influence rather than a loving friend.

DOING YOUR PART

Influencing my children has become one of my life's greatest motivational factors. Proverbs 17:25 says, "A foolish son is a grief to his father, and bitterness to her who bore him." I do not want to feel this way about parenthood. Unfortunately, we live in a time where we see a lot of children who are basically raising themselves. We see kids who go to schools that are in dangerous places, with society and friends shaping the next generation. This has inspired me to pray for my kids before they leave the house—it has become part of our relationship. Often I take hold of their hands before they leave the house, praying for the Lord's protection over them. Every time my son, David, goes out he will walk up to me, saying, "Dad, I will be coming back at such-and-such time. I'm going out now." I will then take him by the hand and pray, "Father, in Jesus' name, be with my son tonight. Protect and keep him. Bring him home safely. And Father, in Jesus' name, I pray that he will be an example to those he is with."

great idea

Our words influence our kids tremendously. As parents, who have more maturity in the Lord than our kids, our words should encourage and challenge our kids to think about their actions. If you think your child has made a poor decision, but you do not approach him in a gentle way, most likely he will not receive whatever wisdom you have to offer. Our speech needs to be filled with grace—not provoking a child to wrath. Proverbs 15:1 says, "A gentle answer turns away wrath, but a harsh word stirs up anger." It is not a parent's responsibility to harshly say, "That was a stupid move!" Really, a remark like that does not help a child—it condemns him. We need to be aware of how our speech affects our children, so that we speak words that edify, not that destroy or tear down.

As the years have gone by, I have become more open to criticism from my kids. When I make a mistake and it is brought to my attention, I will apologize and ask my kids to forgive me. Sometimes they may try to pin blame on me when I have come to them with an issue. Usually, I respond by saying, "The issue isn't me at this moment. I won't have you twisting this around so that I'm the issue." Redirecting their comments, I focus on their behavior. If there is validity to one of my child's comments— though it may hurt—I will ask the Lord to search my heart and show me if I have sinned. When Paul was speaking to the Corinthians he said that he would not judge himself and that it was a small thing if others judged him.

I think we have to allow our children to be children, and also realize that we have not been perfect parents. As we have attempted to do the best that we can, we must rest in our efforts in Christ Jesus and trust Him to help us to sort out the other things. If we have done evil towards our children, we need to confess it and ask for forgiveness. It is important to sit your child down and, without using excuses, explain how you have failed. Chuck Swindoll once pointed out that children are the most forgiving people in the world—I agree with him.

By being open with your family, by letting them see that you make mistakes and that you seek forgiveness, you are giving them more than a long lecture ever could. By being the leader and taking responsibility for your actions, you are living above reproach—not perfectly, but graciously. The Lord promises to exalt those who humble themselves. If we keep this in mind, we will have far greater influence in our children's lives than if we are to conceal all of our mistakes. It is in how we deal with our own lives that we will gain a position of influence in their lives. Since they will choose whom to listen to, forming their own opinions, we should all the more seek to live godly lives before them—that we might influence them to follow after the Lord.

THE TOOLS OF THE TRADE

Regardless of what stage you are in with your children, you will be an instrument in God's hand to mold and shape their lives. But we cannot wait until they are eighteen to become strong, godly influences—we have to start early. Of course, not everyone is a Christian when his or her children are young; however, God is fully capable of restoring the years when He was not first in the home. Parenting is the work of the Spirit. He restores, renews, and refreshes us to do His will. For us to be Spirit-filled parents, we will have to be submitted to the Spirit of God, who gives us the power to parent His way. No mother or father can live out 1Corinthians 13 love apart from the Spirit. If we want to be filled with the Spirit, we will have to abide in Christ—really, this is the greatest skill a parent can acquire. No, we will never be perfect and, yes, we will make mistakes; but we cannot allow our mistakes to overwhelm us, believing that we cannot be effective in our children's lives. Condemnation will separate us from the work that He wants to do in us and through us. So we must ask the Lord to guard our hearts and minds, trusting that He will use such imperfect vessels as ourselves to accomplish His purposes.

Let me encourage you to commit your works to the Lord. As you do, He will establish your path. In other words, as you access the tools of the trade—reading the Word, praying, being a witness, and remaining in fellowship—God will perfect everything which concerns you and your family. If you have been in a struggle with your children, realize that you do not fight flesh and blood. In the book of Ephesians we read that we are in an unseen battle. The enemy wants to destroy you and your children, but he is helpless against the hand of the Lord. Never listen to Satan, who wants to disarm you from fighting for your children. God chose you—He will use you.

Thus, we need to prepare ourselves daily by clothing ourselves with the whole armor of God. Be alert to the devices that Satan uses in your life and in the lives of each family member (1 Peter 5:8). Take up His Word to shield your heart and your mind (Ephesians 6:16). Learn to put off the old man and put on the new man in Christ by allowing the Spirit to renew your mind (Ephesians 4:22–24). If you struggle to show agape love while carrying out parental duties, seek the Lord and ask Him to give you His heart. It is of utmost importance to know and obey God's Word.

Pray strenuously for your children every day. Praying is invading the invisible. Try using Scripture to formulate prayers for your children. Pray specifically for their struggles, and pray for their futures. I pray for my children's future spouses. I want each of my children to marry believers, who will encourage them in their spiritual lives. Pray that they will catch the values that you have modeled for them. We read in 1 Timothy 4:12, "Be an example to the believers in word, in conduct, in love, in spirit, in faith, in purity." Pray that you can live this kind of humility out before your children, in all circumstances. "Meditate on these things; give yourself entirely to them, that your progress may be evident to all" (1 Timothy 4:15). When you give your life entirely over to the service of the Lord and are obedient to His Word, your progress will be evident—your children will see it and God will be glorified!

As seasons come to an end between you and your child, new ones lie ahead. Cherish what God has given you together now. Let me encourage you to communicate with your children while they are still in your care. Instruct them about who they are in Christ. Take every opportunity to tell them that you love them, being open and available to communicate with them about their needs. If they are not walking closely with the Lord, do not be condemned. Trust that your obedience and prayers are effective, remembering that as you are submitted to the Lord, the blood of Christ covers your life. You can entrust your children to His care—they are His gifts, not your possessions.